STEP-UP

ART AND DESIGN

Objects and Meanings

Susan Ogier

Published by Evans Brothers Limited
2A Portman Mansions
Chiltern Street
London W1U 6NR

Produced for Evans Brothers Limited by
White-Thomson Publishing Ltd,
Bridgewater Business Centre,
210 High Street,
Lewes, East Sussex BN7 2NS

Printed in Hong Kong by New Era Printing Co. Ltd

Project manager: Rachel Minay

Designer: Leishman Design

British Library Cataloguing in Publication Data

Ogier, Susan

Objects and Meanings – (Step-up Art & Design)

1. Art and design – (Juvenile literature)

I. Title

372.5'2

ISBN 978 0237 535 766

Acknowledgements: Special thanks to Mrs Pat Allen and the teachers and pupils in Years 3, 4, 5 and 6 at St Luke's Primary School, Kingston upon Thames, Surrey, for all their artwork and help in the preparation of this book.

Picture acknowledgements: Alamy: page 24r (Dod Miller). Bridgeman Art Library: pages 4l (Oscar Reinhart Foundation, Winterhur, Switzerland), 4r (Samuel Courtauld Trust, Courtauld Institute of Art Gallery), 6 (National Gallery, London, UK), 8br (Lefevre Fine Art Ltd. London), 10b (Johnny van Haeften Gallery, London, UK), 12 (National Gallery, London, UK), 16 (Museo Archeologico Nazionale, Naples, Italy), 18 (Indianapolis Museum of Art, USA, Marian and Harold Victor). Corbis: pages 8l (The Gallery Collection), 17 (Macduff Everton), 22l (Enzo & Paolo Ragazzini), 22r (Philadelphia Museum of Art), 26l (Bettmann). Giorgio de Chirico: page 26r. Marcel Duchamp: page 24l. Chris Fairclough: cover (main), title page, pages 5, 7l&r, 9 (all), 11 (all), 15t, 19b, 21 (all), 25, 27, 29r. Istockphoto: pages 10t, 13 (all), 20cl, 20cr&b, 29l. Shutterstock: cover tl (Vankina), cover tr (Julien Tromeur), pages 8tr (Andrew Skinner), 14 (all), 15bl&r, 19t, 20tl, 20bl&c, 20tr, 23 (Neil Roy Johnson), 28 (all).

Contents

What is a still life?

A still life is a work of art that shows a group of inanimate objects (objects that do not live or move). These could be natural objects, such as fruit, flowers, bones or shells, or made objects, such as crockery or fabric. The objects chosen are often taken from everyday life, so looking at a still life can help us learn about the way people live and about their relationship with the world.

Arranging a still life

The artist will usually arrange the objects in a special composition. Sometimes this will be simply for aesthetic reasons – because the arrangement looks pleasing or beautiful. At other times, the artist might want to catch the viewer's interest by placing an item in a strange way, or by putting unusual items together.

▼ *These paintings are* Still Life with Slices of Salmon *by Francisco Jose de Goya and* Still Life with Plaster Cast *by Paul Cezanne. Why do you think the artists chose these objects? Do you think the items have been carefully placed or are they in random positions?*

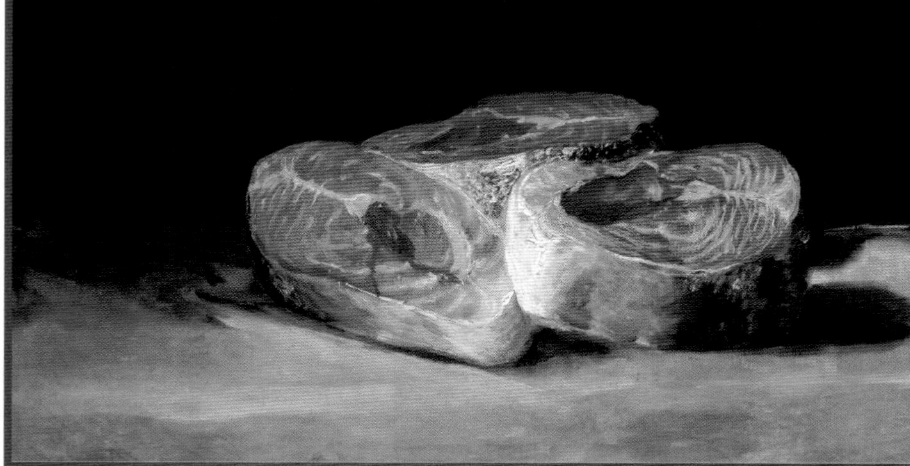

Choosing objects for a still life

Look around your school, home or in the environment for objects you would like to use in a still life. Think about why you have chosen them. Which qualities attracted you to these objects? Do you like their shapes or textures? Perhaps they have bumpy surfaces or bright colours.

Arrange your objects into interesting compositions. Think about their height and width. Try walking around the composition to see where the best viewpoint is. Do you need to create a base underneath to display the objects better within the arrangement? Try different arrangements until you are happy with the result.

Sort and classify

What kinds of objects have your friends chosen? Are they similar to or different from your choices? Can you sort the objects into different groups? Think of imaginative ways to classify the items.

What do objects mean to us?

Artists often include objects in a composition to give information or clues about someone or something. Looking at the objects in a painting can help us learn how people lived in the past and find out what was important to them. Many portraits are good examples of this. The sitter, who may have commissioned the work, might want anyone looking at the painting to know or believe certain things about him or her.

▲ *Have you spotted the fruit near the window? Oranges were a real luxury at this time and would have been very expensive. What does this tell you?*

The Arnolfini Portrait

See what objects you notice in this portrait of Giovanni Arnolfini and his wife. How has the artist, Jan van Eyck, arranged the objects around the figures? Do some of them look as though they have been just left there? Think about how long it takes to create a painting such as this. Do you think it is possible the objects were casually placed?

A mystery?

Why do you think there are two pairs of shoes lying on the floor in the Arnolfini portrait? Make up a story or drama that explains their presence...

What do objects say about you?

Collect items that show aspects of your personality, or say something about your life. Make small sketches in your sketchbook of some of the items. You could use a viewfinder to help you isolate a section to sketch.

Anzul has cut a hole in a piece of card to make a viewfinder. When you are making small sketches, a viewfinder can make it easier for you to choose what to sketch.

Using a source of light, such as a window, place your objects so that light falls across them. Using tone in your drawings and including the shadows that you see will help make your work look more three-dimensional.

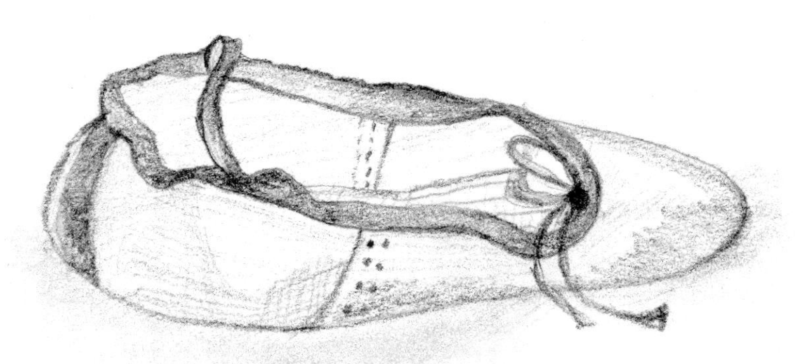

What does this beautifully drawn shoe tell us about the owner? Use your imagination to create a personality profile by asking questions such as: What music would she like? Which would be her favourite colour?

Personality outline

Ask a friend to draw your outline on to a large piece of paper. Fill the outline with images that are special to you. These could include pictures of your family and your favourite activities, as well as paintings, drawings and photographs of objects that mean something to you. You could try to use a colour scheme that you think represents your personality.

Colour, shape and composition

Every work of art can be described in terms of its formal elements (see box). The artist may use these elements singly or in combination.

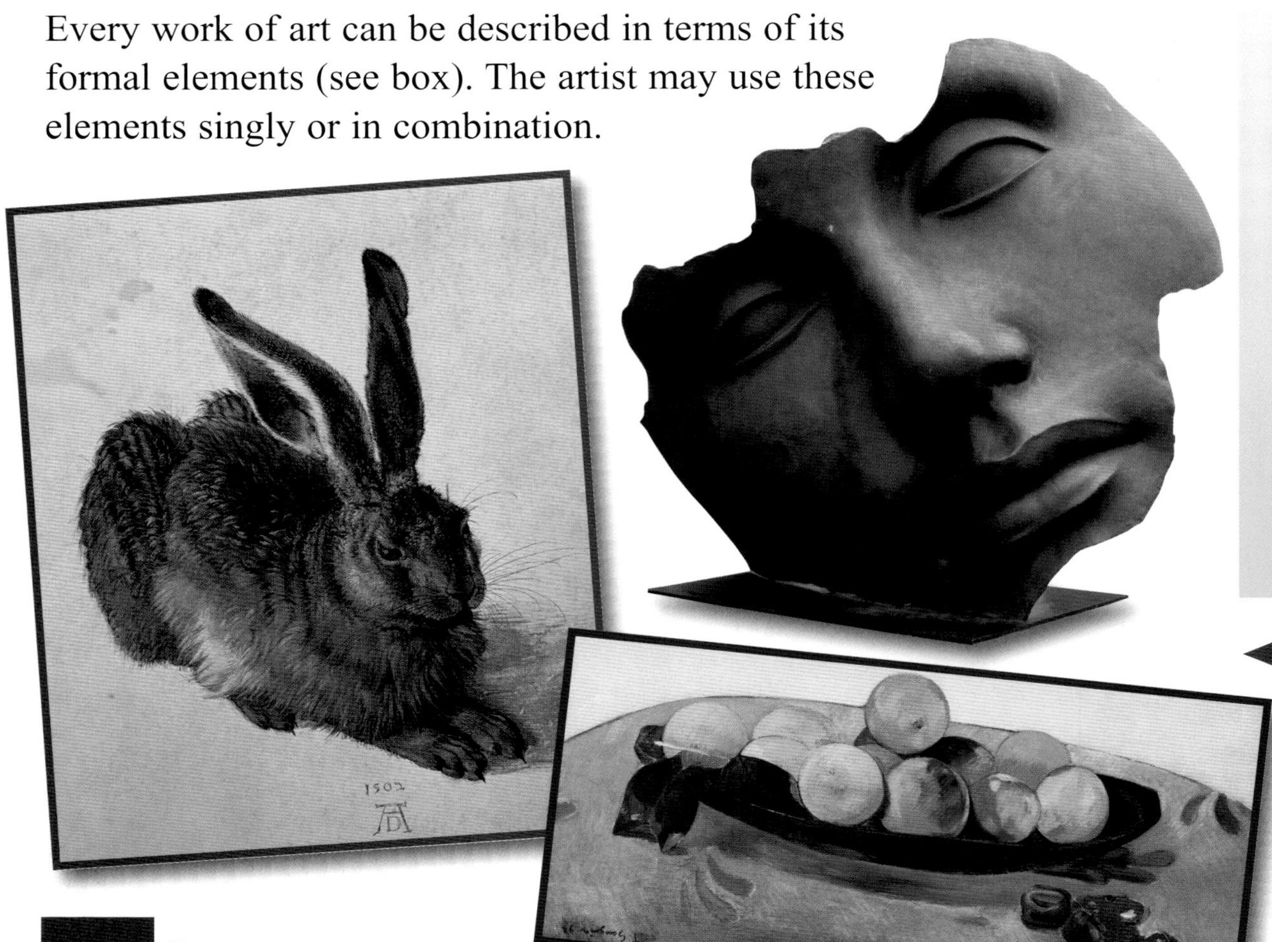

The formal elements of art

- Line
- Tone
- Colour
- Shape
- Space
- Form
- Pattern
- Texture

◀ *Which of the formal elements do you think are most noticeable in each of these works of art?*

Matisse vs Morandi

Go to http://www.museomorandi.it/english/museo/dipinti_aper.htm and http://www.ibiblio.org/wm/paint/auth/matisse/ to compare the works of Henri Matisse and Giorgio Morandi. Matisse makes use of vivid, contrasting colours. How does it make you feel when you look at these bright colours? How do you feel when looking at Morandi's subtle tones? Perhaps you are more interested in the shapes that you can see?

Using colour and shape

Using brightly coloured fabric and objects, set up a still life. First decide on a colour scheme by trying combinations of colour families in your sketchbook using soft or oil pastels. Will you choose complementary colours that clash and contrast or harmonious colours that sit well together?

Concentrate on the shapes of your objects. With charcoal, try drawing the outlines only of the different shapes without looking down or taking your charcoal off the surface of the paper.

▼ *Emily is drawing overlapping outlines of the shapes she sees. Working in this way can create interesting abstract images.*

Refer to your sketchbook's colour scheme to help you complete the painting.

▲ *Emily and Jack have mixed primary colours to fill the shapes.*

Keep standing back to review your painting while you are working on it. At the end, decide what you will do to improve your work next time.

Vanitas

Vanitas vanitatum omnia vanitas

This Latin phrase is from the Bible and means 'Vanity of vanities, all is vanity' or 'Utterly meaningless! Everything is meaningless'.

Humans share the same fate as all life on Earth, which is that our lives must, at some point, come to an end. This is something that has fascinated artists for centuries, and they have explored this idea through still-life paintings in a genre known as 'vanitas'. This type of work was popular in the 17th century and people at that time must have enjoyed searching for meanings in artwork.

This 17th-century painting is Vanitas Still Life by Pieter Claesz. The artist has chosen to include a skull, an empty candle holder, a glass with its contents spilled and a half-peeled, decaying fruit. How do these objects relate to the vanitas theme?

Objects and symbols

Vanitas paintings include certain kinds of objects to represent the passing of time or to show how transitory, or short, human life is. How might an open book with its pages turning, a burning or extinguished candle or an empty cup be symbolic of this theme?

Digital vanitas

Create a still-life display with a vase of beautiful flowers as the focal point. Take it in turns to photograph the flowers over a period of time with a digital camera or video recorder.

Make an exhibition of your investigative work by placing the photographs in a sequence. Ask visitors that come to your exhibition what this work makes them think about.

▼ *What happens to the shapes and colours as the days go by?*

Contemporary art

Look at the video piece *Still Life* by contemporary artist Sam Taylor-Wood at: http://www.ubu.com/film/tw_still.html

Why do you think the artist chose to include a ballpoint pen in her still-life composition?

The domestic and the everyday

Many artists like to explore the subject of everyday life. We can learn more about our own attitudes and values by thinking about the world in which we live. Looking at domestic life can also tell us about people's feelings and what is important to them.

The Dutch Golden Age

In the 17th century there was what is called a 'Golden Age' in the Netherlands. This was a time of prosperity, with many advances in science and art. A genre of painting that became popular was around the theme of the domestic interior. These paintings show people going about their daily lives and explore the relationship between them and the objects they are using.

Then and now

This 17th-century Dutch painting by Jan Steen is called *A Peasant Family at Meal-time*. Think of your own home at a mealtime – how does this compare to Steen's painting? Imagine you are going to list all the differences and similarities; which list do you think would be the longest? Try it and see – were you right?

▲ *The peasant family in Steen's painting are just about to start their meal. How many objects and pieces of furniture can you spot in this scene? Try to think of some reasons why the artist might have chosen to include these items. Why do you think he has placed some of the items on the floor?*

Make a digital diary

Make a video diary or photographic record of a mealtime in your family. Try to frame the view so that the space inside the room is visible. You could include the food preparation and clearing away afterwards. In class, transfer the video or photos to the computer and use editing software to make an art video or presentation to show at school.

Invite your classmates to ask questions about your work. What do you think went well, and what was more difficult?

I filmed my family preparing for a party and then filmed the party itself. Now I'm editing my film on the computer.

Around the world

Look at this interior from the Middle East. Would you believe that this sitting room, with its carpets and wall hangings, is actually the inside of a tent? Use a library or the Internet to find images of other domestic interiors from around the world.

What differences and similarities do you notice between the examples that you find? How do they compare to your own home?

Take a seat

Some objects are functional, which means that they serve a purpose. Many objects have been specially designed to make our lives easier, and furniture for our homes is one example of this.

Create a collage

Cut out interesting designs of chairs and seating from catalogues and magazines to make a collage in your sketchbook. Think about the colours and designs: a seat's function may be to be sat upon, but what about all of the different reasons for sitting, and places that we sit down? Make notes of your ideas in your sketchbook.

Standing room only

Look back at the painting on page 12. Have you noticed anything missing? The man is the only person sitting down. Why do you think this might be?

▲ *Which of these styles appeals to you? Which chair looks most comfortable?*

Design project

Work with a friend to design a chair for a member of the family in Steen's painting. Think about what sizes will be needed if the chair is to be in proportion with the person that you have chosen. Will the chair simply serve its purpose or do you want to design a real treat of a seat?

Make the structure of your chair by creating shapes with cardboard, chicken wire, plastic sheeting, newspaper and masking tape. Use your imagination and add decorative features, curved arms or elaborate headrests with wire and card.

When they have been painted, display the completed chairs. Invite comments from other children and teachers. Which chair would they choose?

▶ *Cover the model in Modroc and allow this to dry before painting the chair.*

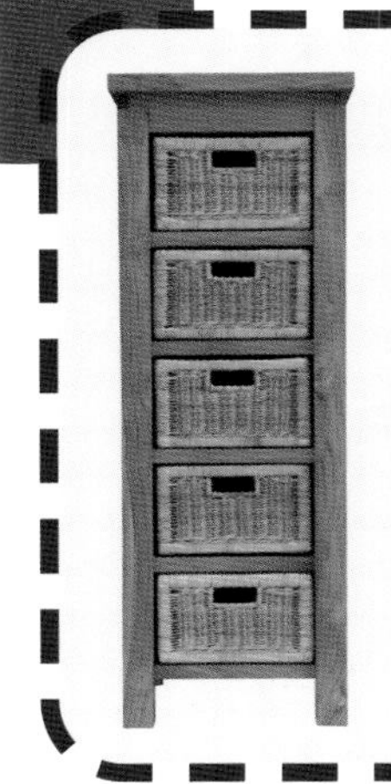

Need or want?

How many different types of furniture can you think of and what are their functions? Which items do you think are essential, and which are less important? For instance, we may need a bed to sleep in, but could probably manage to live without a coffee table or a footstool. Have a class discussion around the subject of needs and wants.

Trompe l'oeil

Ancient civilisations, such as the Greeks and Romans, also included meaningful objects in their art.

Roman frescoes

Evidence of this has been found in representations of everyday objects, such as food items, pitchers (jugs), bowls and musical instruments, that were painted on to the walls of villas at Herculaneum and Pompeii in Italy, towns that were devastated by the volcanic eruption of Mount Vesuvius. These wall paintings are called frescoes and they are around 2,000 years old.

▲ *This fresco from a villa in Pompeii dates from the 1st century. Look how realistic the items in this painting seem. Do you feel as though you could reach in and pick up one of those eggs?*

What is trompe l'oeil?

The frescoes show us how people lived in these ancient civilisations. The surviving paintings are so realistic that they are called trompe l'oeil, which means 'to deceive the eye', as it is sometimes difficult to tell whether the object, or scene, is real or merely a painting.

Trompe l'oeil also occurs in some mosaics that have been excavated by archaeologists.

The Unswept Floor

Go to http://www.artnet.com/Magazine/index/robinson/robinson8-9-1.asp to see an ancient mosaic that was specially created to look like a floor littered with food. What do you think of this mosaic? It seems a little unusual to show discarded bones, leftovers from a meal and natural objects scattered on the floor within a beautifully made piece of art. Do you notice the way that the artist has used the illusion of shadow? What effect does this have on your eye when you look at it?

Map litter hotspots

Take a walk around your school grounds to see where litter has been dropped. Then collect some of the items (wear gloves) or sketch or photograph them.

Create a trompe l'oeil litter map showing where you found the different items. Draw them in detail, using soft pencils, on to a large sheet of paper. Don't forget to show where the shadow falls, to give the illusion of reality.

Display the finished drawing in a communal area and ask children and teachers from other classes to comment on your findings and the resulting artwork.

This amazing trompe l'oeil chalk picture has been drawn directly on to the ground. Could you use chalks to make a picture that would 'deceive the eye' of the viewer?

Containers

Objects found by archaeologists prove that ancient civilisations existed around the world, more than 8,000 years ago in some cases. Many of these items are vessels and other containers and range from elaborate examples found at burial sites to simple items used for daily activities, such as cooking and washing.

Burial finds

Vessels and containers are often found at early burial sites, such as those in China or Egypt. This is because people believed that when they died there was another life for them to go to and they would need to take their possessions and food for the journey with them. The vessels, which are usually made from clay or bronze, would have been filled with food and drink and buried with the dead body.

This bronze container was made in China around 3,000 years ago. What does this tell you about the properties of bronze?

Time capsule

How do you think the objects found at burial sites have survived for so long? What sorts of materials would they have been made from? Think about some of your own possessions. Do you think they will still exist in thousands of years' time? If you could tell people in the future about your life, what would you want them to know?

Choose objects for a class time capsule to plant in your school grounds. Remember to think about the substances the objects are made from.

Draw a modern container

We use all kinds of containers in our daily lives. Collect different examples of containers and draw some of them in your sketchbook. Can you make the container in your drawing look as though it is round and empty? Look carefully at the shapes on the top and bottom of the object in front of you. Use shading to show dark and light areas.

Make a clay pot

Use natural clay or plastic modelling clay to make coil or pinch pots. Add shapes or handles on to it with slip, or make a design by etching into the clay when it is leather hard.

Don't forget that the inside of the pot is important – make some treasures to keep inside your pot with any leftover clay.

Craft containers

The basic design of a container is perhaps one of the most successful designs ever. A container does not need to be beautiful to be useful, but throughout history craftspeople have created vessels and containers in pleasing materials and forms or added decoration to make them more attractive.

Crafts around the world

Research craft containers from different countries. What unusual shapes can you find? What materials have been used? If the work is decorated, is it brightly patterned, such as many Indian crafts, or of a limited palette such as some Aboriginal or African crafts?

Print out pictures from the computer of your favourite designs and stick them into your sketchbook. Write a sentence or two explaining why you have chosen these images; then use coloured pastels or soft pencils to make your own design based on these pictures.

Which of these containers do you like? Are you interested in the patterns and colours or are you more drawn to their shapes? How do you think they would feel to touch?

Make a papier mâché container

Start by making geometric shapes, such as cones, spheres and cubes, with paper and tape.

▶ *Connect the shapes together with tape or glue to form your imaginative container.*

I'm trying to make my container more unusual by adding twists and curls.

▼ *Use brightly coloured tissue and glue to papier-mâché over the whole construction, including on the inside.*

▼ *When you are happy with your container, make it stronger by covering it with PVA glue.*

Folk art objects

Folk art was produced by people, mostly men, who had not been educated in art, but who were skilled tradesmen, or craftsmen, and who used their talents to produce items or record local events. Wood, metal and clay are common materials to be found in folk art and this reflects the down-to-earth qualities of the subject matter.

▼ *This working model of a tricycle is typical of folk art in its use of materials. The figure and tricycle have been carved from wood and the mechanism that makes it go is a rush stem (a grass-like plant).*

▲ *This folk art 'bird tree' is interesting, beautiful and rather funny. Can you try to imagine why a craftsperson might have wanted to make it? What strange but wonderful object would you make?*

Local traditions

Folk art includes the making and decorating of objects in a particular, often rural, community. It reflects the traditions and values of the people who made it and so helps us understand about the history of these small, local communities.

Who were the folk artists?

We do not know the names of many folk artists because the important thing about this type of art is the workmanship and not the artist behind the piece. For instance, a tradesman such as an ironmonger or carpenter might have a sideline in making weather vanes or shop signs. Some folk artists have become famous, for example Alfred Wallis, a Cornish fisherman and artist whose work can now be seen in major galleries.

Grandma Moses

American folk artist Anna Mary Robertson, also known as Grandma Moses, did not start painting until she was in her 70s and carried on until she died aged 101. What else can you find out about Grandma Moses? Put her name into a search engine and find some images of her work.

Colourful canals

One example of folk art is the decorative canal art you might see if you walk along a towpath. These colourful designs, often depicting roses or castles, are painted on anything and everything on the boat, from watering cans to the kitchen sink.

▼ *Have a close look at the colour contrasts on these stylised designs.*

Design idea

Find some old plates, cups or flowerpots on which to paint your own designs using acrylics. What background will you choose and how will the design contrast with that?

Found objects

Some artists include found objects in their work. This means using existing objects as a part of, or as, the artwork. These artworks are sometimes known as 'readymades'.

Daring Duchamp

Marcel Duchamp was an artist who lost interest in painting but became more involved in the concepts, or ideas, that art could stimulate. He made the very first readymade by placing a bicycle wheel upside down on a stool and spinning the wheel around. Duchamp also enjoyed provoking reactions within the art world.

◀ *Duchamp's most famous readymade was a urinal destined for a men's toilet, which he gave the title* Fountain *and entered to an exhibition. His joke caused the reaction that he had hoped for, which was fury among his more traditional colleagues.*

Contemporary art

Contemporary artist Cornelia Parker placed found objects inside a shed and then asked the army to blow the whole thing up. She collected all the pieces to create this artwork, which is made to look as if the shed is still exploding.

▲ *Parker hung the found objects around a light bulb, creating beautiful shadows all around the room.*

The natural environment

Look around your garden, a park or a beach for some interesting natural found objects. Take photographs or make drawings of the objects in their natural habitat so that you can replace them when you have finished with them. Take care not to collect anything that is still growing.

▼ *These children have recreated a woodland scene by using recycled and natural materials and clay to make items that they found on a trip to their local park.*

Installation art

Make an art installation using some natural objects. An installation allows viewers to experience the art all around them by walking right into it, like walking into a room.

Try to think of other things to include in the installation that would encourage viewers to think about the environment, and how we can help to look after it.

Extraordinary objects

Have you ever wondered where ideas come from? Try to think about a time when you had a new thought, or understood something for the first time. Do you remember feeling excited or wanting to share your thought with someone?

The physicist Albert Einstein said: 'Imagination is more important than knowledge. Knowledge is limited. Imagination encircles the world.' What do you think this means? Do you agree with him?

Inspiring ideas

Looking at art from the past can inspire artists and designers to create their own brand new ideas in the same way. The results are what we see in galleries, shops and public spaces.

Whether you are an artist or a designer, you will need to have a very questioning mind, and always be open to thoughts that may seem strange at first.

Dreamlike art

The painting on the right is by Giorgio de Chirico and shows a plaster-cast head, a ball and a rubber glove pinned to a building. The shadows make the mood in the picture seem strange and the sizes of those objects, in relation to the street scene, also appear very peculiar. Why do you think de Chirico has placed these objects together in this way? Perhaps it reminds you of a dream?

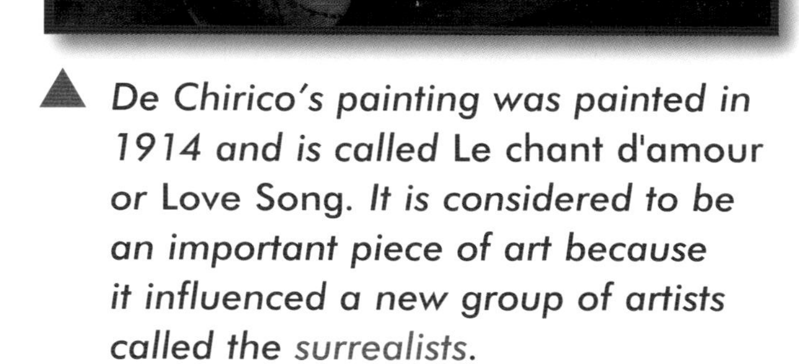

De Chirico's painting was painted in 1914 and is called Le chant d'amour *or* Love Song. *It is considered to be an important piece of art because it influenced a new group of artists called the* surrealists.

Mini-installation

Find three unrelated objects and arrange them together to make a mini-installation on a tabletop. Use some large cardboard sheets, paint and drawing materials to create a background for your piece.

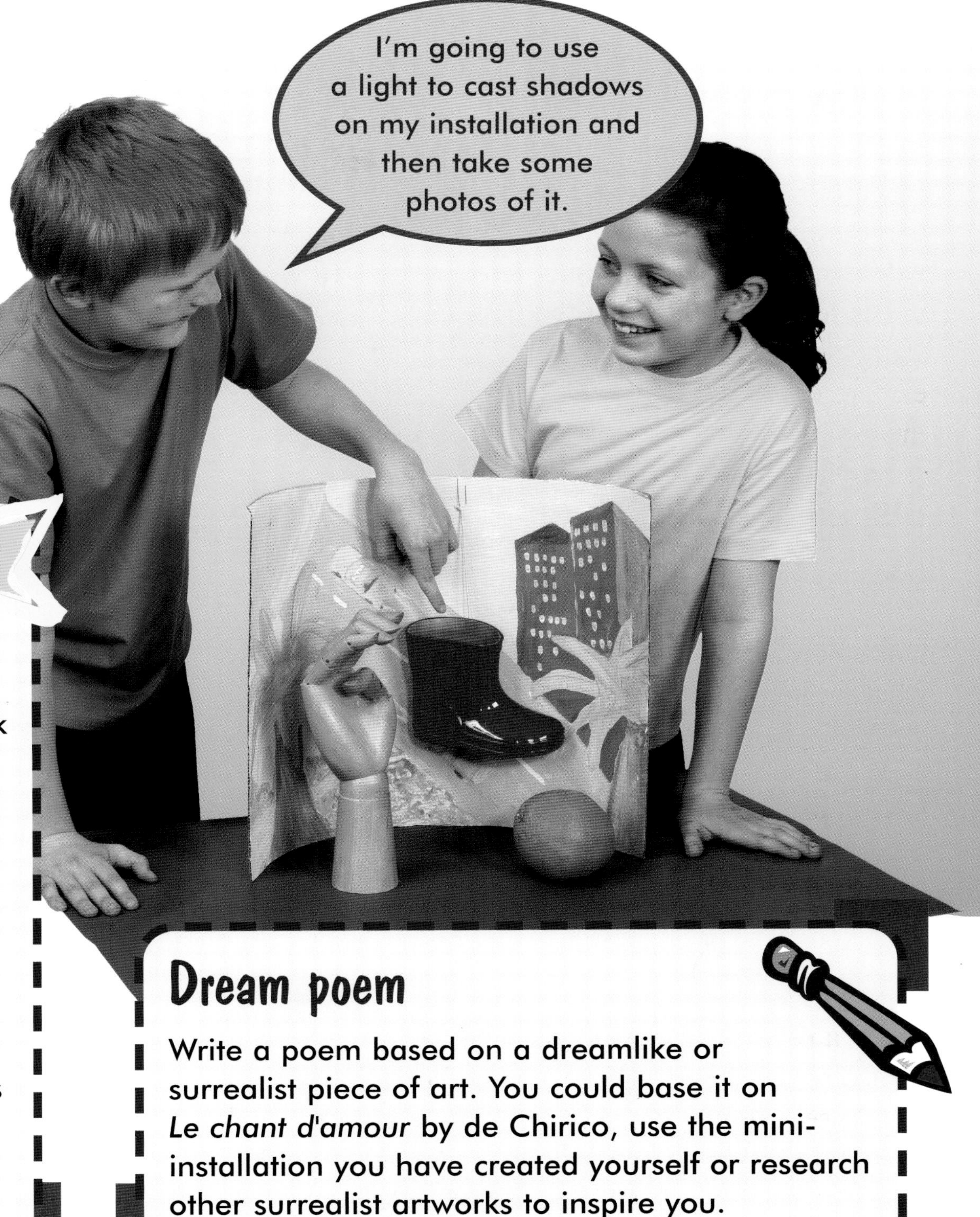

What's your invention?

Place some ordinary objects into a bag and ask a friend to take two out. Try to invent a brand-new object by combining characteristics from the two items that have been selected. To make it harder, try the same activity with three objects.

Draw your new inventions and carry out some research to test whether they would really work.

Dream poem

Write a poem based on a dreamlike or surrealist piece of art. You could base it on *Le chant d'amour* by de Chirico, use the mini-installation you have created yourself or research other surrealist artworks to inspire you.

Glossary

abstract describes artwork that is not obviously a picture of something.

acrylic a thick, plastic-based paint. Make your own by adding PVA glue to poster paint.

aesthetic relating to beauty.

archaeologist a person who investigates ancient objects to find out about past civilisations.

civilisation a particular society at a particular time and place. We usually think of a civilisation as having developed to an advanced stage.

classify to divide into groups.

collage an artwork made by sticking images or fabrics on to a flat surface.

colour family the different shades of one colour, for instance a red colour family might include raspberry and maroon.

commission ask an artist to create an artwork, usually in return for payment.

complementary used to describe colours that provide good contrasts when placed next to one another, for example yellow and purple.

composition the arrangement of different elements to create a complete artwork.

contemporary of the same time or period. In this context it means the present day.

domestic interior the inside of a house.

etching drawing on to something by pressing or scratching into its surface.

focal point the place in a work of art that grabs the viewer's attention.

fresco a wall painting. Traditionally frescoes were painted on to damp plaster and so became part of the plaster, rather than just being painted on top.

genre the category of a style of art.

geometric relating to geometry. Geometry is the area of mathematics that deals with lines, angles and shapes.

habitat the natural home or environment of a plant or animal.

harmonious used of colours that seem to 'go together', for instance, green, blue and purple.

illusion something that looks real but is not.

in proportion — the right size compared to the size of something else.

leather hard — used of clay that has partly dried. You can scratch into the surface of leather-hard clay, but it is not wet enough to be moulded into a shape.

limited palette — only a few particular colours.

mosaic — a picture or design made from small pieces of glass or stone.

oil pastel — a medium that has the texture of a wax crayon, but which allows colours to be blended more easily, especially when a little oil is added.

property — a basic characteristic.

quality — a characteristic.

random — used to describe things that are placed or happen by chance.

rural — characteristic of the countryside.

shadow — the dark area that is cast where light is blocked by an object.

sketchbook — a plain paged book an artist uses to keep visual information to use another time. A sketchbook can be used for note taking, memory jogging, to solve problems or experiment with ideas and techniques.

slip — clay that has been dissolved in water so that it can be used as a glue to join two pieces of clay together.

soft pastel — a powdery, coloured art medium.

stylised — in this context, uses a well-recognised format for making designs.

subtle — used to describe a very slight change in something.

surrealists — a group of artists interested in dreams and the subconscious mind.

symbolic — used where an image of one thing stands for another thing, for example a heart shape is used to mean 'love'.

texture — the feel of a surface.

three-dimensional — having height, width and depth.

tone — the lightness, darkness or quality of colour.

vessel — a container, usually round and mostly used for holding liquids.

viewer — the person who is to look at the work.

viewfinder — a tool for isolating a small area from a larger view.

viewpoint — the direction from which you look at something.

For teachers and parents

This book is designed to cover the learning objectives of the QCA Schemes of Work for Art and Design in KS2. Its aim is to provide imaginative and contemporary ways of working with the schemes. Specifically it covers Unit 5C Objects and Meanings, but essential elements of Units 4B Take a Seat and 5B Containers are also included.

Children might have already experienced Unit 1B Investigating Materials, 1C What is Sculpture? and 3B Investigating Pattern.

The ideas and activities are designed to act as starting points for deeper investigation and, in line with the programmes of study, it should be remembered that all the activities take place within the process of:

- Exploring and developing ideas.
- Investigating and making art, craft and design.
- Evaluating and developing work.
- Developing knowledge and understanding.

SUGGESTED FURTHER ACTIVITIES

Pages 4 - 5 What is a still life?
The objects in a still life can come from nature or from the made world. Any item from the real world could be used, perhaps related to topic work or guided by the children's interest. See http://www.tate.org.uk/learnonline/ for online information and help.

Encourage the children to think about their personal relationships with objects. The objects chosen might reflect things that they value and which can demonstrate their own relationship with the world. Asking children to make their own still-life arrangements will engage them emotionally with the task and enable them to develop a sense of ownership over the final artwork.

Teach the children to view their arrangements from every direction, so they develop a sense of seeing something from another perspective. The more practice they have at this, the more they will develop an intuitive sense of balance and symmetry.

Find out more about Cezanne at: http://www.metmuseum.org/explore/cezannes_apples/splash.html and more about Goya at: http://eeweems.com/goya/index.html

Pages 6 - 7 What do objects mean to us?
Children could do the personality outline activity shown here and then display these as class 'portraits'. Can other children and parents tell which portrait belongs to which child?

Objects in works of art can help us reflect upon attitudes and values in society and culture. You might develop the idea of how we place value on certain things but not on others. What would the children think of as valuable? What do we mean by 'value'?

Pages 8 - 9 Colour, shape and composition
Matisse's painting *Le Bateau* hung upside down in the Museum of Modern Art, New York, for two months before anyone noticed. Ask the children why they think this might have happened. Go to http://www.theapesheet.com/archive/newart2.html to see the upside-down version of Matisse's painting and discover which works by other famous artists have also been hung incorrectly. Find out more about Georgio Morandi at: http://www.tate.org.uk/modern/exhibitions/morandi/

Remind children of their previous learning before you start the activity on this page. Demonstrate the principles of colour mixing on the interactive whiteboard: http://www.ngflcymru.org.uk/vtc/colour_mixing/eng/Introduction/default.htm

Pages 10 - 11 Vanitas
Vanitas means 'everything is pointless'. Ask the children how they feel about this as an idea and develop a philosophical discussion through circle time activities around this theme.

Explain that this type of work was popular in the 17th century and people might have spent a great deal of time looking at the works of art to work out what they mean. How does this compare to the sorts of things we enjoy doing today? Do any of the children enjoy working out puzzles in their spare time? Put it to the children that this might have been a 17th-century alternative to television.

A good interactive game around this theme can be found at: http://www.tate.org.uk/kids/mementomori/

Pages 12 - 13 The domestic and the everyday
Put this painting by Steen into its historical context by reminding children of their Year 2 history topic, (Unit 5). One year or so after this

painting was made the Great Fire of London destroyed four-fifths of the city but only killed 16 people.

Go to http://www.tate.org.uk/imap/imap2/index.html, part of Tate's access for visually impaired people, for a selection of modern and contemporary works that explore the theme 'The Everyday Transformed'.

For more information and images of domestic interiors, have a look at the website http://www.rca.ac.uk/csdi/didb/ and type 'images' into the search facility.

Pages 14 - 15 Take a seat
Ask the children if they think that it is fair that the father sits first. Or should parents put their children's needs before their own? Or is it necessary for parents to look after their own needs first, so that they are fit enough to care for their children? You could have a debate at circle time on this issue.

Play 'What if...' games with the children to encourage creative thinking skills. 'What if... we were born with chairs already attached?' Can you think of any advantages or disadvantages for this scenario?

After completing the design project, encourage the children to write a short drama based on the work to perform at a parents' assembly. It could explain why the family had only one chair, but now, thanks to them, has more than enough. How will having more chairs change their lives?

Pages 16 - 17 Trompe l'oeil
Some examples of Greek and Roman frescoes and mosaics are available at: http://www.metmuseum.org. Follow the links to Greek and Roman Art.

Link a project on Roman art to history, geography and science by investigating volcanoes. Go to http://www.sciencenewsforkids.org/articles/20060315/Note3.asp for a starting point for looking at Mount Vesuvius and science-based interactive games. See how one class created models of volcanoes that erupt at http://www.rochedalss.qld.edu.au/vesuvius/eruption.htm
You could arrange a school trip to visit one of Britain's Roman excavation sites such as Fishbourne or Bignor.

Pages 18 - 19 Containers
Find images of Ancient Chinese burial vessels at http://www.comptonverney.co.uk and learn more about the ancient Egyptians at http://www.ancientegypt.co.uk

Talk to the children about the shapes on a round vessel and teach them to draw an ellipse to describe the rim of a cup or vase. The shape will be similar at the base of the object too. Observing geometric shapes in objects during art can provide children with a practical application for work in maths (Shape, Space and Measures).

Pages 20 - 21 Craft containers
The British Museum has a whole section on 'Containers' to explore. It includes images, ideas and activities as well as a downloadable teacher's pack. Go to:
http://www.britishmuseum.org/explore/families_and_children/online_tours/containers/containers.aspx
Other sites to look at for images of crafts from around the world are:
http://www.indianetzone.com/crafts/ and
http://www.african-art-and-crafts.com/
Look at the finished articles with your class. Ask the children which objects are particularly successful and why they think that is. Ask them how they could have improved their own pieces of work.

Pages 22 - 23 Folk art objects
Britain's largest collection of folk art online is at:
http://www.comptonverney.org.uk/?page=collections/britishFolkArt

When the children have finished their work, help them display it by creating your own folk art museum. Staple cardboard boxes on to a display board and disguise them with tissue paper before placing the children's work on to them. Discuss with your class which colours in the paintings contrast well with the chosen backgrounds. What changes could they have made to have improved their designs?

Pages 24 - 25 Found objects
Learn all about Duchamp and view images at:
http://www.understandingduchamp.com/

The sculptures of contemporary artist Richard Wentworth incorporate objects directly from the real world. Some images are available at Tate Online. The images at http://www.core77.com/reactor/03.07_parallel.asp show how Wentworth comes across art in everyday life. This notion could be developed in the classroom by discussion followed by a photography project.

Pages 26 - 27 Extraordinary objects
Playing with extraordinary ideas can lead to surprising new inventions that are of great value to us. Encourage children to think of what they consider to be the most important inventions in our history.

Index